A RESOURCE FOR PARENTS & CHILDREN
GOING THROUGH A LOSS

But,
Where
is Heaven?

BY
JEN TRUSSELL

Published by
Hasmark Publishing, judy@hasmarkservices.com

Illustrator:
Mickey Eves
mickey.eves@sympatico.ca

Design & Layout,
Anne Karklins
annekarklins@gmail.com

ISBN-13: 978-1-988071-97-8
ISBN-10: 1988071976

Hasmark
PUBLISHING

This book is dedicated to Taylor and Emily,
who have stretched my soul farther than I could have
ever imagined. Your wisdom and love carry me
through all of life's adventures.

Mommy, I am sad.

Grandma is gone
    and I don't know
how to find her.

Oh, Sweetheart,
    Grandma died and
lives in heaven now.

But Mommy,
       where IS heaven?

Well Sweetheart,
       Heaven is a lot of
different places.

Heaven is like
a magic garden…

With beautiful flowers, fluffy
clouds, endless tables
of food, rainbows, unicorns,
and elves.

Or heaven is like…

A space within the stars,
with comets, milky ways,
twinkling stars, moonbeams,
and stardust!

And heaven is like...

A beautiful beach, with endless sky, shining sun, waves, dolphins jumping, birds singing and kids playing on the beach.

Mommy?
   Can I talk to Grandma
at her new home?

Of course Sweetheart,
   you can talk to her
anytime you like.

And will she answer me?

You will hear her answers
in the breeze, in a bird's
song, in the flutter of a
butterfly's wings or your
favourite music.

Mommy, heaven sounds
beautiful, can I go visit?

Well, heaven is somewhere
you go when you die,
when your time on Earth
is done.

But there is a way.

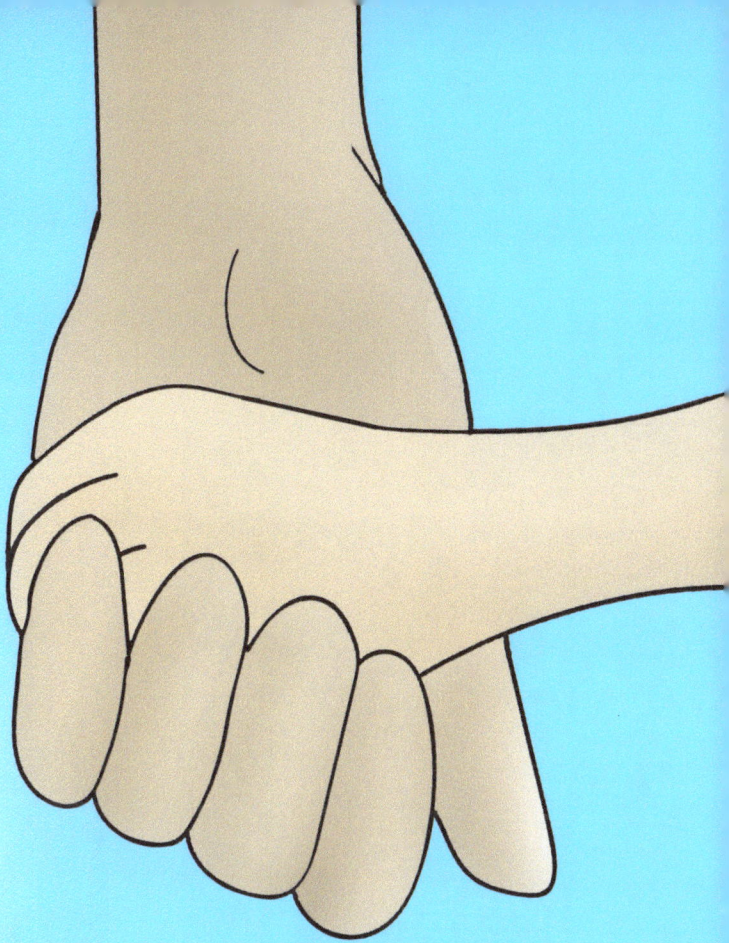

The way you can visit heaven
is through your heart
or in your imagination.

Hmm, Ok.
    But Mommy?

Yes Sweetheart?

I am still sad.

I know so am I. It will
    take some practice to
get used to heaven as
    her new home.

Ok Mommy,
    will you help me?

Of course,
    we can do this together.

I love you.

Tips for Parents

Grief is a transformation and it will take practice to become used to your new routine and life after a loss. Be gentle with yourself in thoughts and actions. Here are a few tips that will help you practice with your children.

- ➤ Be clear about what you believe happens when we die.
- ➤ Use words that accurately describe the situation like dead and died. Avoid words like "she's sleeping"
- ➤ Talk when your child wants to talk, cry when they want to cry, be open about your feelings, especially if your child asks.
- ➤ Continue to use your loved one's name in conversation to avoid making it a taboo subject or suppressing feelings of sadness.
- ➤ Keep the conversation age appropriate but do not hide what is going on because your child is young.

Follow Up Activities for Kids

- ➤ Draw a picture of what you think heaven looks like
- ➤ Draw or write a goodbye picture/letter to go with grandma

Note to the Reader

We have used "Mommy" and "Grandma" for this book. However please feel free to use whatever name is appropriate to your situation at the time to make the story more personal and meaningful.

About the Author

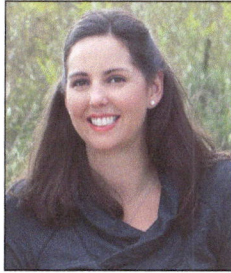

My superpower is embracing my dark side, mirroring it in others and transforming sadness into hope for a new future.

I am a 5th generation Funeral Director, and I grew up in a Funeral home – yes like "My Girl"! After University, I completed my Funeral Service Education Degree at Humber College in 2002 and became a licensed Funeral Director in 2004 and currently still hold a valid license. I continued to work in Toronto for almost 10 years at some of the busiest funeral homes in the city, working closely with families experiencing trauma and transition.

In 2012, I completed my Yoga Teaching Training; I have studied Energetics and Intuition with Karen Strumos, Intuitive Medium, and discovered more of my magic with the beautiful Asha Frost, Healing Rainbow Medicine Woman. In 2013, I developed a Holistic Grief Yoga Program. I love to help people during their grieving journey. If I have learned anything over my life, it is that we never stop learning, even when it feels like we cannot possibly move forward. We can learn, grow, and even heal our past as we learn to live with new life circumstance.

Om. Peace.

Jen

THE LITERARY FAIRIES

We make your literary wish come true!

Jen Trussell

is excited to introduce you to her new friends

The Literary Fairies

TLF is a cool place where you can find out
how YOU could become a published author or
how to help grant a literary wish.
Have an adult visit TLF website for more details
about what we do and how you can help,
and also get your FREE colouring pages
and "fill-in-the-blank story"

http://theliteraryfairies.com/free-for-kids/